English

This book is designed to help young children develop basic English skills. The lessons reinforce phonics skills, sequencing skills, and lead to a better understanding of word usage. Children are introduced to nouns, verbs, and adjectives, homonyms, antonyms and synonyms. They also learn how and when to use capitalization and how to organize words within a sentence. As with the other books in the English Skills Series, all of these exercises provide practice in the skills that can lead to a more thorough understanding of the English language.

Table of Contents

1

Copyright© 1995 American Education Publishing Co.

Table of Contents (continued)

Glossary

ABC Order: Putting objects or words in the same order in which they appear in the alphabet.

Antonyms: Words that are opposites.

Asking Sentence: An asking sentence begins with a capital letter, ends with a question mark and asks a question.

Beginning Consonants: Sounds that come at the beginning of words that are not vowel sounds. (Vowels are the letters a, e, i, o, u and sometimes y.)

Capital Letters: Letters that are used at the beginning of names of people and places. They are also used at the beginning of sentences. These letters (**A B C D E F G H I J K L M N O P Q R S T U V W X Y Z**) are sometimes called the "big" letters.

Compound Words: When two words are put together to make one word. Example: house + boat = houseboat.

Describing Words: Words that tell us more about a person, place, or thing.

Ending Consonants: Sounds, which are not vowel sounds, that come at the end of words.

Homonyms: Words that sound the same but are spelled differently and mean different things. Example: blue and blew.

Nouns: Words that tell the names of persons, places or things.

Sound Discrimination: Being able to identify the differences between sounds.

Super E: When you add an **e** to some words and the vowel changes from a short vowel sound to a long vowel sound. Example: rip + **e** = **ripe**.

Synonyms: Words that mean the same thing. Example: small and little.

Telling Sentences: These sentences begin with a capital letter, end with a period and tell us something.

Verbs: Words that tell what a person or thing can do.

Word Order: The logical order of words in sentences.

Copyright© 1995 American Education Publishing Co.

Name: _____

ABC Order

Directions: Draw a line to connect the dots. Follow the letters
in **ABC** order.

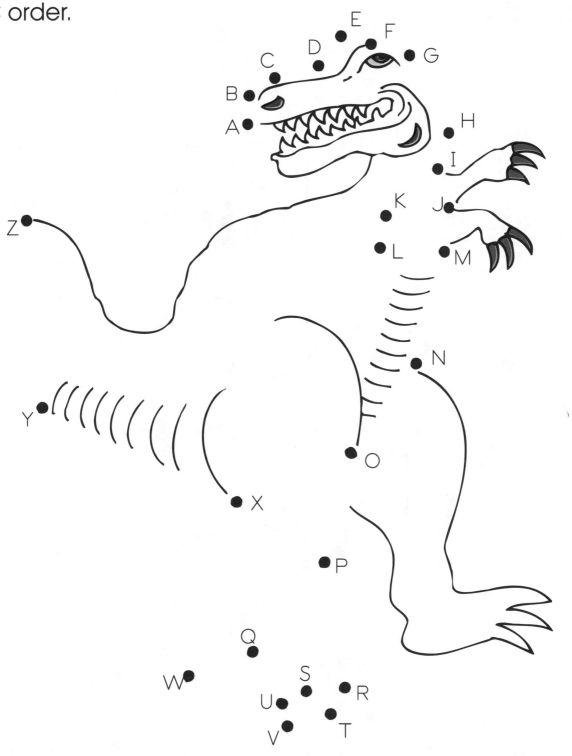

Copyright© 1995 American Education Publishing Co.

Name: _____

abc Order

Directions: Draw a line to connect the dots. Follow the letters in **abc** order.

Name: _____

Beginning Consonants Bb, Cc, Dd, Ff

Beginning consonants make the sounds that come at the beginning of words. Consonants are the letters b, c, d, f, g, h, j, k, l, m, n, p, q, r, s, t, v, w, x, y, z.

Directions: Say the name of each letter. Say the sound each letter makes. Draw a circle around the letters that make the beginning sound for each picture. Say the name of someone you know whose name begins with each letter.

Bb   Cc   Dd   Ff

Bb Dd   Ff Cc   Cc Dd   Ff Bb

Bb Dd   Ff Cc   Cc Dd   Ff Bb

Copyright© 1995 American Education Publishing Co.

Name: _____

Beginning Consonants Gg, Hh, Jj, Kk

Directions: Say the name of each letter. Say the sound that each letter makes. Then, trace the letter that makes the beginning sound in the picture. After you finish, look around the room. Name the things that start with the letters Gg, Hh, Jj, and Kk.

Gg   Hh   Jj   Kk

Kk   Hh   Gg   Kk

Gg   Hh   Jj   Gg

Copyright© 1995 American Education Publishing Co.

Name: _____

Beginning Consonants Ll, Mm, Nn, Pp

Directions: Say the name of each letter. Say the sound each letter makes. Then, trace the letters. Now, draw a line from each letter to the picture which begins with the letter. After you finish, say the letters Ll, Mm, Nn, Pp again.

Ll   Mm   Nn   Pp

Ll

Mm

Nn

Pp

Copyright© 1995 American Education Publishing Co.

Name: _____

Beginning Consonants Qq, Rr, Ss, Tt

Directions: Say the name of each letter. Say the sound that each letter makes. Then, trace each letter in the boxes. Color the picture which begins with the sound of the letter.

Qq   Rr   Ss   Tt

Copyright© 1995 American Education Publishing Co.

Name: _____

Beginning Consonants Vv, Ww, Xx, Yy, Zz

Directions: Say the name of each letter. Say the sound the letter makes. Then, trace the letters. Now, draw a line from the letters that match the beginning sound in each picture.

V v   W w   X x   Y y   Z z

V v

W w

X x

Y y

Z z

Copyright© 1995 American Education Publishing Co.

Review

Directions: Help Meg and Kent and their dog, Sam, get to the magic castle. Trace all of the letters of the alphabet. Then, write the lower case consonant next to the matching upper case letter on the road to the magic castle. Make the sound for each consonant. After you finish, draw a picture on another paper of what you think Meg and Sam will find in the magic castle.

V__ W__ Y__ Z__
X__

T__

S__

R__ P__ M__ K__

Q__ N__ L__ J__

H__

G__

C__ F__

B__ D__

Copyright© 1995 American Education Publishing Co.

Name: _____

Ending Consonants b, d, f

Ending consonants are the sounds that come at the end of the words that are not the vowel sounds.

Directions: Say the name of each picture. Then, write b, d, or f to name the ending sound for each picture.

Copyright© 1995 American Education Publishing Co.

Name: _____

Ending Consonants g, m, n

Directions: Say the name of the picture. Draw a line from each letter to a picture which ends with the sound of that letter.

g   m   n

g

m

n

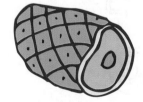

Copyright© 1995 American Education Publishing Co.

Name: _____

Ending Consonants k, l, p

Directions: Say the name of the pictures. Color the pictures in each row that end with the sound of the letter at the beginning of the row. Trace the letters.

 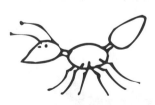   

Copyright© 1995 American Education Publishing Co.

Name: _____

Ending Consonants r, s, t, x

Directions: Say the name of the picture. Then circle the ending sound for each picture.

   r s t x      r s t x

   r s t x      r s t x

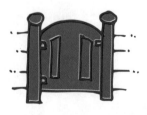   r s t x      r s t x

   r s t x      r s t x

Copyright© 1995 American Education Publishing Co.

Name: _____

Beginning and Ending Sounds Discrimination

Directions: Say the name of the picture. Draw a blue circle around the picture if it begins with the sound of the letter. Draw a green triangle around the picture if it ends with the sound of the letter.

w

l

m

k

n

u

t

s

z

15

Copyright© 1995 American Education Publishing Co.

Name: _____

Beginning and Ending Sounds Discrimination

Directions: Say the name of each picture. Draw a triangle around the letter that makes the beginning sound. Draw a square around the letter that makes the ending sound. Color the pictures.

o   r   t   f   d   w   v   t   b

x   c   r   t   g   d   d   a   k

l   m   h   x   g   r   p   t   v

Copyright© 1995 American Education Publishing Co.

Name: _____

Beginning and Ending Sounds Discrimination

Directions: Look at the example. Say the beginning and ending sounds for the word **pipe**. Write the letter that makes the beginning and ending sound for each picture.

p   p ___

___      ___

___   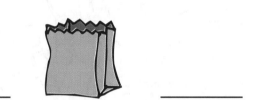   ___

___      ___

___      ___

___   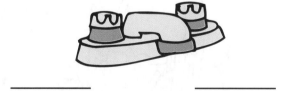   ___

___      ___

___      ___

Copyright© 1995 American Education Publishing Co.

Name: _____

Review

Directions: Say the name of each object which has a consonant near it. Color the object orange if it begins with the sound of the letter. Color the object purple if it ends with the sound of the letter.

Copyright© 1995 American Education Publishing Co.

18

Name: _____

Short Vowel Sounds

The short vowel sounds used in this book are found in the following words: ant, egg, igloo, on, up.

Directions: Say the name of each picture. The short vowel sound may be in the front of the word or in the middle of the word. Color the pictures in each row that have the correct short vowel sound.

a				
e				
i				
o				
u				

19

Copyright© 1995 American Education Publishing Co.

Name: _____

Long Vowel Sounds

Long vowel sounds say their own name. The following words have long vowel sounds: hay, me, pie, no, cute.

Directions: Say the name of each picture. Color the pictures in each row that have the correct long vowel sound.

a

e

i

o

u

Copyright© 1995 American Education Publishing Co.

20

Name: _____

Discrimination Of Short And Long Aa

Directions: Say the name of each picture. If it has the short ă sound, color it red. If it has the long ā sound, color it yellow.

ă

ā

21

Copyright© 1995 American Education Publishing Co.

Name: _____

Discrimination Of Short And Long Ee

Directions: Say the name of each picture. Draw a circle around the pictures which have the short **ĕ** sound. Draw a triangle around the pictures which have the long **ē** sound.

ĕ   ē

Copyright© 1995 American Education Publishing Co.

Name: _____

Discrimination Of Short And Long Ii.

Directions: Say the name of each picture. Color it yellow if it has the short **i** sound. Color it red if it has the long **ī** sound.

ī̠   ı̆

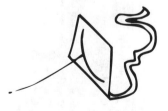

Copyright© 1995 American Education Publishing Co.

Name: _____

Discrimination Of Short And Long Oo

Directions: Say the name of each picture. If the picture has a long **o** sound, write a green **L** in the space. If the picture has a short **o** sound, write a red **S** in the space.

_____

_____

_____

_____

_____

_____

_____

_____

Copyright© 1995 American Education Publishing Co.

Discrimination Of Short And Long Uu

Directions: Say the name of the picture. If it has the long **u** sound, write a **u** in the unicorn column. If it has a short **u** sound, write a **u** in the umbrella column.

Copyright© 1995 American Education Publishing Co.

Name: _____

Short And Long Vowel Sounds

Directions: Say the name of the picture. Write the correct vowel on each line to finish the word. Color the short vowel pictures yellow. Circle the long vowel pictures.

  j _____ g

 t _____ pe

 l _____ af

  p _____ n

 l _____ ck

 c _____ t

 c _____ be

  b _____ ll

 k _____ te

 r _____ pe

Copyright© 1995 American Education Publishing Co.

Name: _____

ABC Order

Use the first letter of each word to put the words in alphabetical order.

Directions: Draw a circle around the first letter of each word. Then, put the words in **ABC** order.

ⓒa r   ⓑi r d   moon   two   nest   fan

bird

car

card   dog   pig   bike   sun   pie

Copyright© 1995 American Education Publishing Co.

Name: _____

ABC Order

Directions: Circle the first letter of each animal's name. Write a 1, 2, 3, 4, 5, or 6 on the line next to the animals' names to put the words in **ABC** order.

skunk _____

dog _____

butterfly _____

zebra _____

tiger _____

fish _____

Copyright© 1995 American Education Publishing Co.

Name: _____

The Super E

When you add an **e** to some words, the vowel changes from a short vowel sound to a long vowel sound.

Example: rip + **e** = ripe.

Directions: Say the word under the first picture in each pair. Then, add an **e** to the word under the matching picture. Say the new word.

pet   _____

tub   _____

man   _____

kit   _____

pin   _____

cap   _____

Copyright© 1995 American Education Publishing Co.

Name: _____

Compound Words

Compound words are two words that are put together to make one word.

Directions: Look at the pictures and read the two words that are next to each other. Now, put the words together to make a new word. Write the new word.

Example:

 + **=**

house **boat**

houseboat

 **+**  **=**

side   walk

lip   stick

 **+**  **=**

sand   box

 **+**  **=**

lunch   box

Copyright© 1995 American Education Publishing Co.

Name: _____

Synonyms

Synonyms are words that mean the same thing. **Start** and **begin** are synonyms.

Directions: Find the two words that describe each picture. Write the words in the boxes below the picture.

small funny large sad silly little big unhappy	

Copyright© 1995 American Education Publishing Co.

Name: _____

Antonyms

Antonyms are words that are opposites. **Hot** and **cold** are antonyms.

Directions: Draw a line between the words that are opposites. Can you think of other words that are opposites?

closed

below

full

empty

above

old

new

open

Copyright© 1995 American Education Publishing Co.

Name: _____

Homonyms

Homonyms are words that sound the same but are spelled differently and mean something different. **Blew** and **blue** are homonyms.

Directions: Look at the word pairs. Choose the word that describes the picture. Write the word on the line next to the picture.

1. sew   so   _____

2. pair   pear   _____

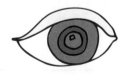

3. eye   I   _____

4. see   sea   _____

Copyright© 1995 American Education Publishing Co.

Name: _____

Review

Directions: Read the sentences below. Fill in the blanks with the correct word. Then circle the first letter of each word and write them in **ABC** order on the lines below.

| sunglasses | Pete | rock | cold | eight |

1. Sun + glasses = _____.

2. Another word for stone is _____.

3. The opposite word for hot is _____.

4. A word that sounds like the word ate _____.

5. Add an "e" to the word pet _____.

ABC Order: _____ _____ _____

_____ _____ _____

_____ _____ _____

_____ _____ _____

_____ _____ _____

Copyright© 1995 American Education Publishing Co.

Name: _____

Nouns Are Naming Words

Nouns tell the name of a person, place, or thing.

Directions: Look at each picture. Color it red if it names a person. Color it blue if it names a place. Color it green if it names a thing.

35

Copyright© 1995 American Education Publishing Co.

Name: _____

Nouns Are Naming Words

Directions: Write these naming words in the correct box.

store	zoo	child	baby	teacher	table
cat	park	gym	woman	sock	horse

Person _____ _____

Place _____ _____

Thing _____ _____

Copyright© 1995 American Education Publishing Co.

More Than One

Some nouns name more than one person, place or thing.

Directions: Add an "s" to make the words tell about the picture.

frog___

pan ___

boy ___

egg___

horn ___

girl ___

Copyright© 1995 American Education Publishing Co.

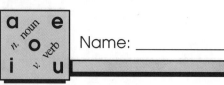

Name: _____

More Than One

Directions: Read the nouns under the pictures. Then, write the noun under **One** or **More Than One**.

One

_____

_____

_____

_____

_____

_____

More Than One

_____

_____

_____

_____

_____

_____

barn

cows

ducks

wagon

horse

pigs

Copyright© 1995 American Education Publishing Co.

Verbs Are Action Words

Verbs are words that tell what a person or a thing can do.

Example: The girl pats the dog.
The word "pats" is the verb. It shows action.

Directions: Draw a line between the verbs and the pictures that show the action.

eat

run

sleep

swim

sing

hop

Copyright© 1995 American Education Publishing Co.

Verbs Are Action Words.

Directions:
Look at the pictures.
Read the words.
Write an action
word in each
sentence below.

1. The two boys like to _____ together.

2. The children_____ the soccer ball.

3. Some children like to _____ on the swings.

4. The girl can_____ very fast.

5. The teacher_____ the bell.

Copyright© 1995 American Education Publishing Co.

Name: _____

Is And Are Are Special Words

Use "is" when talking about one person or one thing. Use "are" when talking about more than one person or thing.

Example: The dog is barking.
The dogs are barking.

Directions: Write "is" or "are" in the sentences below.

1. Jim_____ playing baseball.

2. Fred and Sam _____ good friends.

3. Cupcakes _____ my favorite treat.

4. Lisa _____ a good soccer player.

Copyright© 1995 American Education Publishing Co.

Name: _____

Nouns And Verbs

Directions: Read the sentences below. Draw a red circle around the nouns. Draw a blue line under the verbs.

1. The boy runs fast.

2. The turtle eats leaves.

3. The fish swim in the tank.

4. The girl hits the ball.

Copyright© 1995 American Education Publishing Co.

Name: _____

Words That Describe

Describing words tell us more about a person, place, or thing.

Directions: Read the words in the box. Choose a word that describes the picture. Write it next to the picture.

happy	round	sick	cold	long

_____

_____

_____

_____

_____

_____

_____

_____

_____

_____

_____

_____

_____

Copyright© 1995 American Education Publishing Co.

Name: _____

Words That Describe

Directions: Read the words in the box. Choose the word that describes the picture. Write it on the line below.

wet	round	funny	soft	sad	tall

_____   _____

_____   _____

_____   _____

Copyright© 1995 American Education Publishing Co.

Name: _____

Words That Describe

Directions: Circle the describing word in each sentence. Draw a line from the word to the picture.

1. The hungry dog is eating.

2. The tiny bird is flying.

3. Horses have long legs.

4. She is a fast runner.

5. The little boy was lost.

Copyright© 1995 American Education Publishing Co.

Name: _____

Names Of People

The names of people begin with a capital letter.

Directions: Choose a name from the box to go with each child. Write the name on the line. Start each name with a capital letter.

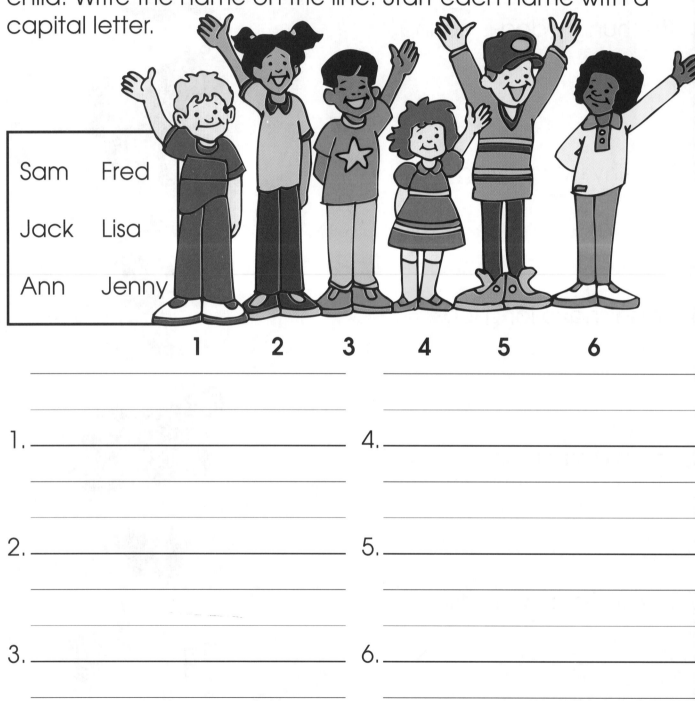

Sam	Fred
Jack	Lisa
Ann	Jenny

1   2   3   4   5   6

1. _____

2. _____

3. _____

4. _____

5. _____

6. _____

Copyright© 1995 American Education Publishing Co.

Name: _____

Name That Cat

The name of a pet begins with a capital letter.

Directions: Read the names in the box. Choose one name for each cat. Write the name in the space under the cat.

Fritz	Fuzzy	Boots	King	Queenie	Lola

_____   _____   _____

_____   _____   _____

_____   _____   _____

_____   _____   _____

Copyright© 1995 American Education Publishing Co.

Name: _____

Holidays

Holidays begin with capital letters.

Directions: Choose the words from the box to match the holiday. Write the words under the picture. Be sure to start with capital letters.

| Fourth of July President's Day | Valentine's Day Thanksgiving |

_____

_____

_____

_____

_____

_____

_____

_____

Copyright© 1995 American Education Publishing Co.

Days of the Week

The days of the week begin with capital letters.

Directions: Write the days of the week in the spaces below. Put them in order. Be sure to start with capital letters.

Tuesday

Saturday

Monday

Friday

Thursday

Sunday

Wednesday

Copyright© 1995 American Education Publishing Co.

Name: _____

Review

Directions: Circle the letters that should be capital letters. Underline the describing words.

1. jan has red flowers for mother's day.

2. We eat a hot lunch on monday.

3. jim and fred are fast runners.

4. spot is a small dog.

5. We go to the big store on friday.

Copyright© 1995 American Education Publishing Co.

Name: _____

Telling Sentences

Sentences can tell us something. Telling sentences begin with a capital letter. They end with a period.

Directions: Read the sentences. Draw a yellow circle around the capital letter at the beginning of the sentence. Draw a purple circle around the period at the end of the sentence.

1. I am seven years old.

2. The bird is pretty.

3. The boy likes to dance.

4. Turtles like to swim.

Copyright© 1995 American Education Publishing Co.

Name: _____

Telling Sentences

Directions: Read the sentences. Write the sentences on the lines below. Begin each sentence with a capital letter. End each sentence with a period.

1. most children like pets
2. some children like dogs
3. some children like cats
4. some children like snakes
5. some children like all animals

1. _____

_____

2. _____

_____

3. _____

_____

4. _____

_____

5. _____

_____

Copyright© 1995 American Education Publishing Co.

Name: _____

Telling Sentences

Directions: Read the sentences. Write the sentences below. Start each sentence with a capital letter and end with a period.

1. i like to go to the store with Mom
2. we go on Friday
3. i get to push the cart
4. i get to buy the cookies
5. i like to help Mom

1. _____

_____

2. _____

_____

3. _____

_____

4. _____

_____

5. _____

_____

Copyright© 1995 American Education Publishing Co.

Asking Sentences

Asking sentences ask a question. An asking sentence begins with a capital letter. It ends with a question mark.

Directions: Draw a green line under the sentences that ask a question.

1. Does your room look like this?

2. Are the walls yellow?

3. There are many children.

4. Do you sit at desks or tables?

5. The teacher likes her job.

Copyright© 1995 American Education Publishing Co.

Name: _____

Asking Sentences

Directions: Draw a blue line under the sentences that ask a question.

1. We like to camp.

2. Do you like to camp?

3. We like to sing at camp.

4. Can you make a fire?

5. We like to cook hot dogs.

Copyright© 1995 American Education Publishing Co.

Name: _____

Asking Sentences

Directions: Write the first word of each asking sentence. Be sure to start each question with a capital letter. End each question with a question mark.

1. _____ you like the zoo   **do**

2. _____ much does it cost   **how**

3. _____ you feed the ducks   **can**

4. _____ you see the monkeys   **will**

5. _____ time will you eat lunch   **what**

Copyright© 1995 American Education Publishing Co.

Name: _____

Periods And Question Marks

Use a period at the end of a telling sentence. Use a question mark at the end of an asking sentence.

Directions: Put a period or a question mark at the end of each sentence below.

1. Do you like a parade

2. The clowns lead the parade

3. Can you hear the band

4. The balloons are big

5. Can you see the horses

Copyright© 1995 American Education Publishing Co.

Name: _____

Review

Directions: Look at the picture. In the space below, write one telling sentence about the picture. Then, write one asking sentence about the picture.

A telling sentence.

_____

_____

_____

An asking sentence.

_____

_____

_____

Copyright© 1995 American Education Publishing Co.

Name: _____

I Can Write Sentences

Directions: Draw a picture of yourself in the box marked **Me**. Then write three sentences about yourself on the lines.

Me

[blank box for drawing]

1. _____

2. _____

3. _____

Copyright© 1995 American Education Publishing Co.

Name: _____

Review

Directions: Put the words in the right order to make a sentence. The sentences will tell a story.

1. a gerbil. has Ann
2. is The Mike. named gerbil
3. likes eat. Mike to
4. play. to Mike likes
5. happy a is gerbil. Mike

_____

1. _____

_____

2. _____

_____

3. _____

_____

4. _____

_____

5. _____

_____

Copyright© 1995 American Education Publishing Co.

In My Home

Do this with a grown-up.
Look around your home.

Mitt begins with the same sound as **moon.**

Find something that begins with the same sound as <u>run</u>.

Write its name. _____
Draw a picture of what you named.

Find something that begins with the same sound as <u>ball</u>.

Write its name. _____
Draw a picture of what you named.

Find something that ends with the same sound as <u>wet</u>.

Write its name. _____
Draw a picture of what you named.

Find something that ends with the same sound as <u>good</u>.

Write its name. _____
Draw a picture of what you named.

Suitcases

Do this with a grown-up.

Help the Green family pack for a trip.

Take turns.

Draw a line from each person to things
he or she will pack.

Mom will pack things with names that begin with
the same sound as <u>mop</u>.

Dad will pack things with names that begin with
the same sound as <u>pig</u>.

Pat will pack things with names that end with
the same sound as <u>look</u>.

Bill will pack things with names that end with
the same sound as <u>well</u>.

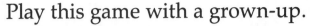

Toss a Word

Play this game with a grown-up.

Get a penny and toss it on the game board.

Look at the letter in the space where the penny lands.

Try to use the letter to finish a word on your

Word Card.

Write the letter in the word.

Take turns.

To win, you must fill in your Word Card first.

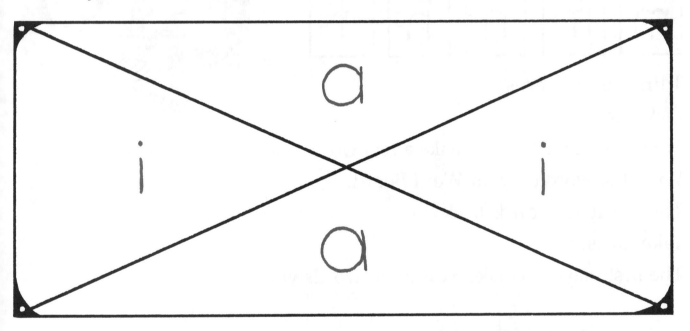

My Word Card

l___p   d___g   r___b   c___p   f___n   m___p

My Grown-up's Word Card

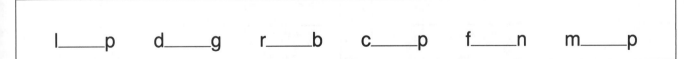

l___p   d___g   r___b   c___p   f___n   m___p

Make a Word

Play this game with a grown-up.
Make letter cards like these.

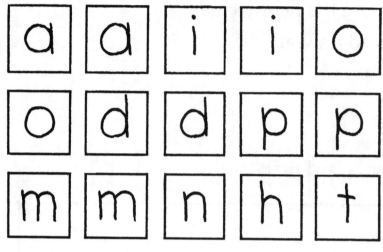

Turn over the cards.

Pick 3 cards.

Try to use the letters to make a real word.

Write the word on your Word Board.

Then turn your cards back over.

Take turns.

The first player to make 3 different words wins.

My Word Board	**My Grown-up's Word Board**

Do They Sound the Same?

Play this game with a grown-up.
Make word cards like these.

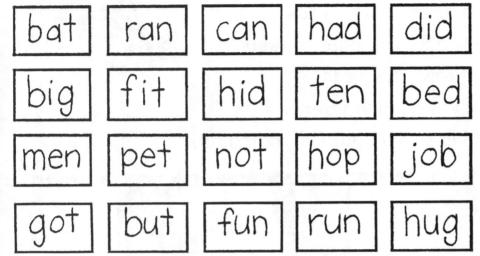

bat	ran	can	had	did
big	fit	hid	ten	bed
men	pet	not	hop	job
got	but	fun	run	hug

Turn over the cards.

Pick 2 cards.

Read the words on the cards out loud.

Listen for the vowel sounds.

If the words have the same vowel sound,
keep the cards.

If the words do not have the same vowel sound,
turn the cards back over.

Take turns.

Play until no more cards are left.

Then count your cards.

How many cards do you have? _____

How many cards does your grown-up have? _____

The player with more cards wins the game.

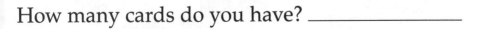

Word Checkers

Play this game with a grown-up.

Make 8 small red markers.

Put them on the two bottom rows of words.

Have your grown-up make 8 small blue markers.

Put them on the two top rows of words.

Then play checkers, but with one difference.

Read the word in a box before you put a marker on it.

	to		do		has		of
let		as		so		fly	
	us		for		be		old
two		now		who		way	
	get		me		by		yes
up		had		her		him	
	but		old		saw		day

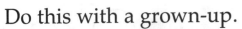

Which Is Better?

Do this with a grown-up.

Read the words in the first box.

Put an **X** under the name of the thing you like better.

Put a ✔ under the name of the thing your grown-up likes better.

Do the rest of the boxes the same way.

apple or banana	milk or juice	lions or tigers
elephants or bears	trees or flowers	winter or summer
airplanes or trains	cars or trucks	orange or green

Make up 2 more sets of words.

Put an **X** under the names of the things you like better.

_____ or _____   _____ or _____

Fill the Balloons

Play this game with a grown-up.

Toss a coin on the game board.

Read the words in the box where the coin lands.

If the words have the same or almost the same meaning, color 2 of your balloons.

If the words have opposite meanings, color 1 balloon.

Take turns.

You win if you color all your balloons first.

happy	on	little	more
sad	off	small	less
nice	silly	up	below
mean	funny	down	under

My Balloons

My Grown-up's Balloons

Identifying synonyms and antonyms

ANSWER KEY

MASTER ENGLISH
1

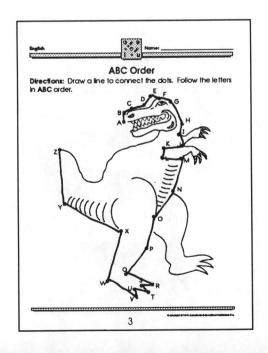

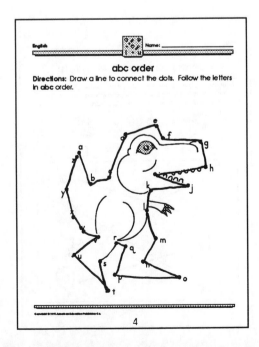

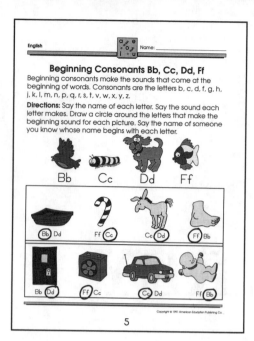

Beginning Consonants Bb, Cc, Dd, Ff

Beginning consonants make the sounds that come at the beginning of words. Consonants are the letters b, c, d, f, g, h, j, k, l, m, n, p, q, r, s, t, v, w, x, y, z.

Directions: Say the name of each letter. Say the sound each letter makes. Draw a circle around the letters that make the beginning sound for each picture. Say the name of someone you know whose name begins with each letter.

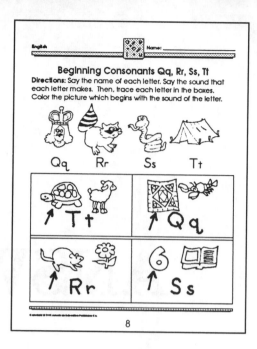

Beginning Consonants Qq, Rr, Ss, Tt

Directions: Say the name of each letter. Say the sound that each letter makes. Then, trace each letter in the boxes. Color the picture which begins with the sound of the letter.

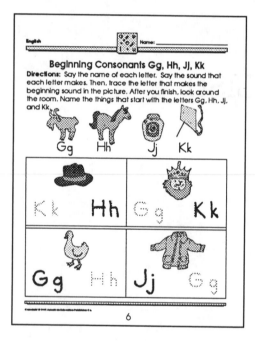

Beginning Consonants Gg, Hh, Jj, Kk

Directions: Say the name of each letter. Say the sound that each letter makes. Then, trace the letter that makes the beginning sound in the picture. After you finish, look around the room. Name the things that start with the letters Gg, Hh, Jj, and Kk.

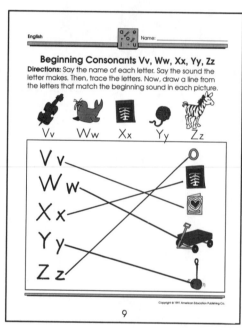

Beginning Consonants Vv, Ww, Xx, Yy, Zz

Directions: Say the name of each letter. Say the sound the letter makes. Then, trace the letters. Now, draw a line from the letters that match the beginning sound in each picture.

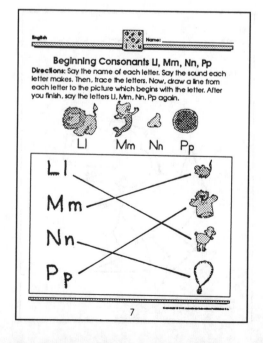

Beginning Consonants Ll, Mm, Nn, Pp

Directions: Say the name of each letter. Say the sound each letter makes. Then, trace the letters. Now, draw a line from each letter to the picture which begins with the letter. After you finish, say the letters Ll, Mm, Nn, Pp again.

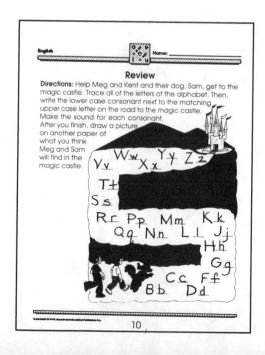

Review

Directions: Help Meg and Kent and their dog, Sam, get to the magic castle. Trace all of the letters of the alphabet. Then, write the lower case consonant next to the matching upper case letter on the road to the magic castle. Make the sound for each consonant. After you finish, draw a picture on another paper of what you think Meg and Sam will find in the magic castle.

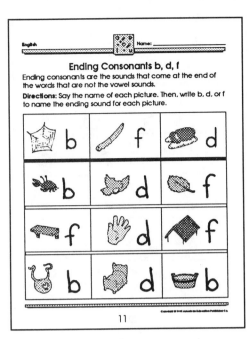

Ending Consonants b, d, f

Ending consonants are the sounds that come at the end of the words that are not the vowel sounds.

Directions: Say the name of each picture. Then, write b, d, or f to name the ending sound for each picture.

b	f	d
b	d	f
f	d	f
b	d	b

11

Ending Consonants r, s, t, x

Directions: Say the name of the picture. Then circle the ending sound for each picture.

r s t x   r s t x

r s t x   r s t x

r s t x   r s t x

r s t x   r s t x

14

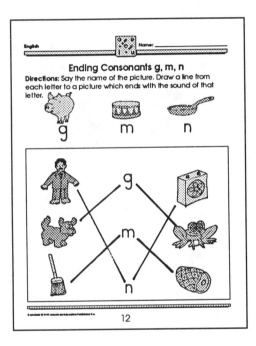

Ending Consonants g, m, n

Directions: Say the name of the picture. Draw a line from each letter to a picture which ends with the sound of that letter.

g   m   n

g
m
n

12

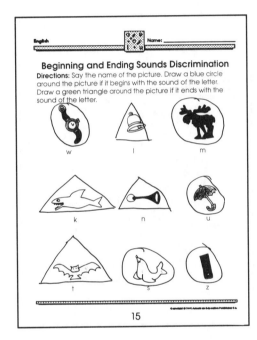

Beginning and Ending Sounds Discrimination

Directions: Say the name of the picture. Draw a blue circle around the picture if it begins with the sound of the letter. Draw a green triangle around the picture if it ends with the sound of the letter.

w   l   m

k   n   u

t   s   z

15

Ending Consonants k, l, p

Directions: Say the name of the pictures. Color the pictures in each row that end with the sound of the letter at the beginning of the row. Trace the letters.

k

l

p

13

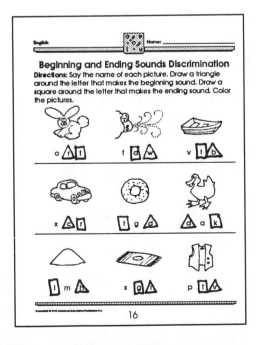

Beginning and Ending Sounds Discrimination

Directions: Say the name of each picture. Draw a triangle around the letter that makes the beginning sound. Draw a square around the letter that makes the ending sound. Color the pictures.

o   r   t   f   c   w   v   t   b

x   c   r   l   g   d   a   a   k

l   m   t   x   q   t   p   t   t

16

75

Beginning and Ending Sounds Discrimination

Directions: Look at the example. Say the beginning and ending sounds for the word **pipe**. Write the letter that makes the beginning and ending sound for each picture.

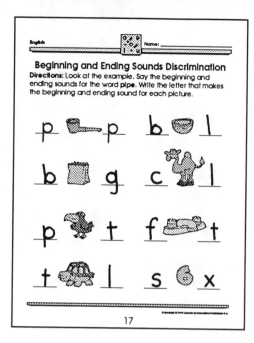

17

Review

Directions: Say the name of each object which has a consonant near it. Color the object orange if it begins with the sound of the letter. Color the object purple if it ends with the sound of the letter.

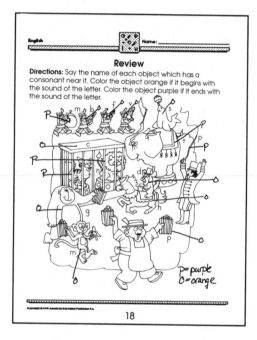

p = purple
o = orange

18

Short Vowel Sounds

The short vowel sounds used in this book are found in the following words: ant, egg, igloo, on, up.

Directions: Say the name of each picture. The short vowel sound may be in the front of the word or in the middle of the word. Color the pictures in each row that have the correct short vowel sound.

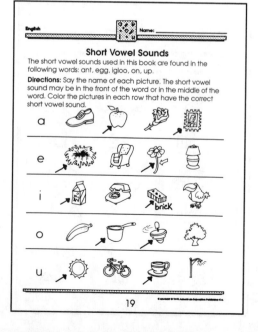

a
e
i
o
u

19

Long Vowel Sounds

Long vowel sounds say their own name. The following words have long vowel sounds: hay, me, pie, no, cute.

Directions: Say the name of each picture. Color the pictures in each row that have the correct long vowel sound.

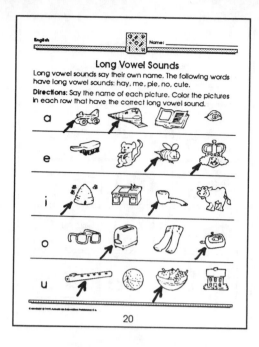

a
e
i
o
u

20

Discrimination Of Short And Long Aa

Directions: Say the name of each picture. If it has the short ă sound, color it red. If it has the long ā sound, color it yellow.

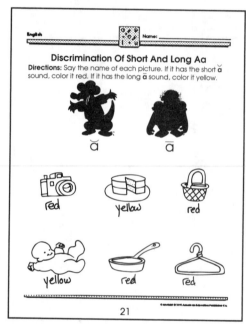

ă   ā

red   yellow   red

yellow   red   red

21

Discrimination Of Short And Long Ee

Directions: Say the name of each picture. Draw a circle around the pictures which have the short ĕ sound. Draw a triangle around the pictures which have the long ē sound.

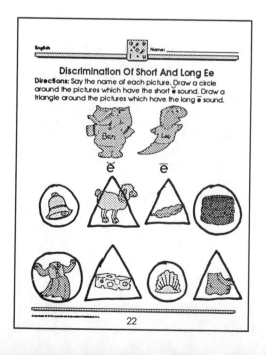

ĕ   ē

22

76

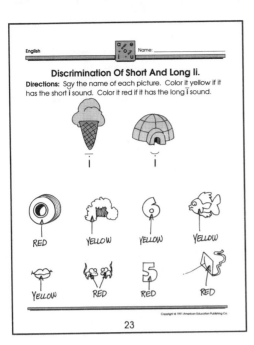

Discrimination Of Short And Long Ii.

Directions: Say the name of each picture. Color it yellow if it has the short i sound. Color it red if it has the long i sound.

RED — YELLOW — YELLOW — YELLOW

YELLOW — RED — RED — RED

23

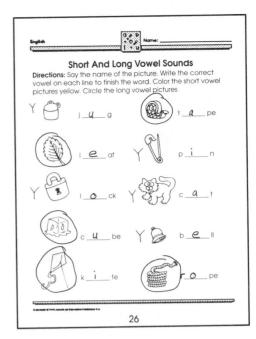

Short And Long Vowel Sounds

Directions: Say the name of the picture. Write the correct vowel on each line to finish the word. Color the short vowel pictures yellow. Circle the long vowel pictures.

Y j _u_ g   t _a_ pe

l _e_ af   p _i_ n

Y l _o_ ck   Y c _a_ t

c _u_ be   Y b _e_ ll

k _i_ te   r _o_ pe

26

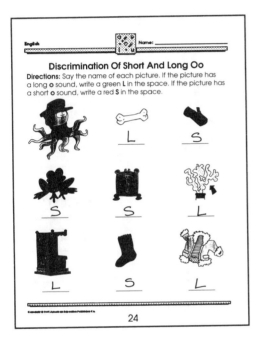

Discrimination Of Short And Long Oo

Directions: Say the name of each picture. If the picture has a long o sound, write a green L in the space. If the picture has a short o sound, write a red S in the space.

L — S

S — S — L

L — S — L

24

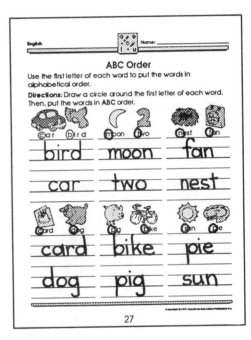

ABC Order

Use the first letter of each word to put the words in alphabetical order.

Directions: Draw a circle around the first letter of each word. Then, put the words in ABC order.

car — bird — moon — two — nest — fan

bird — moon — fan

car — two — nest

card — dog — pig — bike — sun — pie

card — bike — pie

dog — pig — sun

27

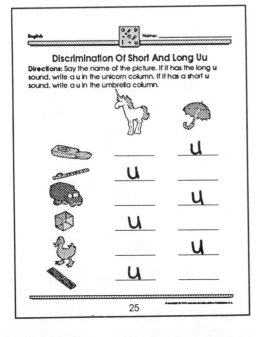

Discrimination Of Short And Long Uu

Directions: Say the name of the picture. If it has the long u sound, write a u in the unicorn column. If it has a short u sound, write a u in the umbrella column.

u

u

u

u

u

25

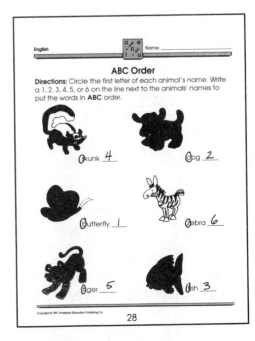

ABC Order

Directions: Circle the first letter of each animal's name. Write a 1, 2, 3, 4, 5, or 6 on the line next to the animals' names to put the words in **ABC** order.

Skunk _4_   Dog _2_

Butterfly _1_   Zebra _6_

Tiger _5_   Fish _3_

28

77

The Super E

When you add an **e** to some words, the vowel changes from a short vowel sound to a long vowel sound.

Example: rip + **e** = ripe.

Directions: Say the word under the first picture in each pair. Then, add an **e** to the word under the matching picture. Say the new word.

pet	*Pete*	tub	*tube*
man	*mane*	kit	*kite*
pin	*pine*	cap	*cape*

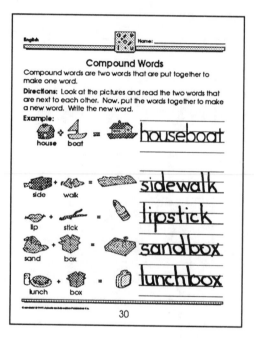

Compound Words

Compound words are two words that are put together to make one word.

Directions: Look at the pictures and read the two words that are next to each other. Now, put the words together to make a new word. Write the new word.

Example:

house + boat = *houseboat*

side + walk = *sidewalk*

lip + stick = *lipstick*

sand + box = *sandbox*

lunch + box = *lunchbox*

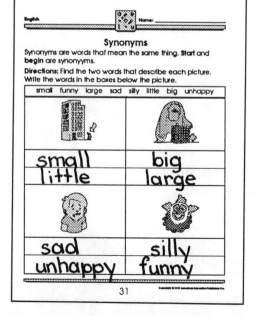

Synonyms

Synonyms are words that mean the same thing. **Start** and **begin** are synonyms.

Directions: Find the two words that describe each picture. Write the words in the boxes below the picture.

small	funny	large	sad	silly	little	big	unhappy

small little	*big large*
sad unhappy	*silly funny*

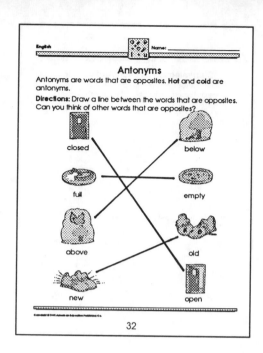

Antonyms

Antonyms are words that are opposites. **Hot** and **cold** are antonyms.

Directions: Draw a line between the words that are opposites. Can you think of other words that are opposites?

closed — below
full — empty
above — old
new — open

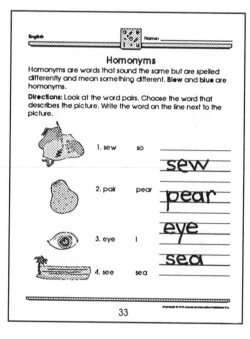

Homonyms

Homonyms are words that sound the same but are spelled differently and mean something different. **Blew** and **blue** are homonyms.

Directions: Look at the word pairs. Choose the word that describes the picture. Write the word on the line next to the picture.

1. sew   so   *sew*
2. pair   pear   *pear*
3. eye   I   *eye*
4. see   sea   *sea*

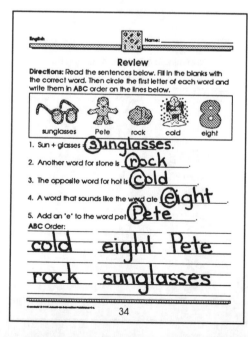

Review

Directions: Read the sentences below. Fill in the blanks with the correct word. Then circle the first letter of each word and write them in ABC order on the lines below.

sunglasses	Pete	rock	cold	eight

1. Sun + glasses ⓢ*unglasses*.
2. Another word for stone is ⓡ*ock*
3. The opposite word for hot is ⓒ*old*
4. A word that sounds like the word ate ⓔ*ight*
5. Add an 'e' to the word pet ⓟ*ete*

ABC Order:

*cold   eight   Pete
rock   sunglasses*

Nouns Are Naming Words

Nouns tell the name of a person, place, or thing.

Directions: Look at each picture. Color it red if it names a person. Color it blue if it names a place. Color it green if it names a thing.

35

More Than One

Directions: Read the nouns under the pictures. Then, write the noun under One or More Than One.

One

barn

wagon

horse

More Than One

cows

ducks

pigs

38

Nouns Are Naming Words

Directions: Write these naming words in the correct box.

store	zoo	child	baby	teacher	table
cat	park	gym	woman	sock	horse

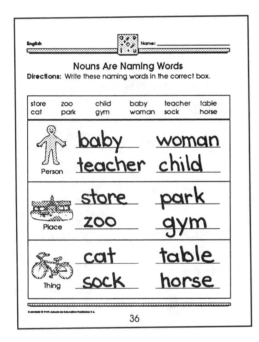

Person: baby · woman · teacher · child

Place: store · park · zoo · gym

Thing: cat · table · sock · horse

36

Verbs Are Action Words

Verbs are words that tell what a person or a thing can do.

Example: The girl pats the dog.
The word "pat" is the verb. It shows action.

Directions: Draw a line between the verbs and the pictures that show the action.

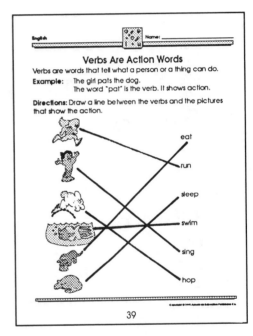

eat

run

sleep

swim

sing

hop

39

More Than One

Some nouns name more than one person, place or thing.

Directions: Add an "s" to make the words tell about the picture.

frog **S**

pan **S**

boy **S**

egg **S**

horn **S**

girl **S**

37

Verbs Are Action Words.

Directions: Look at the pictures. Read the words. Write an action word in each sentence below.

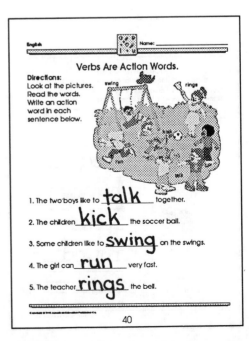

swing

rings

1. The two boys like to **talk** together.

2. The children **kick** the soccer ball.

3. Some children like to **swing** on the swings.

4. The girl can **run** very fast.

5. The teacher **rings** the bell.

40

Is And Are Are Special Words

Use "is" when talking about one person or one thing. Use "are" when talking about more than one person or thing.

Example: The dog is barking.
                The dogs are barking.

Directions: Write "is" or "are" in the sentences below.

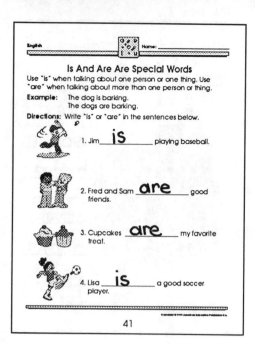

1. Jim __is__ playing baseball.

2. Fred and Sam __are__ good friends.

3. Cupcakes __are__ my favorite treat.

4. Lisa __is__ a good soccer player.

Words That Describe

Directions: Read the words in the box. Choose the word that describes the picture. Write it on the line below.

wet	round	funny	soft	sad	tall

soft   tall

funny   sad

round   wet

Nouns And Verbs

Directions: Read the sentences below. Draw a red circle around the nouns. Draw a blue line under the verbs.

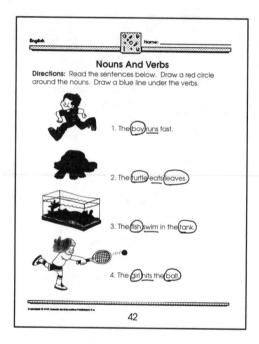

1. The boy runs fast.

2. The turtle eats leaves.

3. The fish swim in the tank.

4. The girl hits the ball.

Words That Describe

Directions: Circle the describing word in each sentence. Draw a line from the word to the picture.

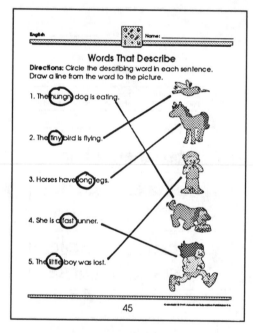

1. The hungry dog is eating.

2. The tiny bird is flying.

3. Horses have long legs.

4. She is a fast runner.

5. The little boy was lost.

Words That Describe

Describing words tell us more about a person, place, or thing.

Directions: Read the words in the box. Choose a word that describes the picture. Write it next to the picture.

happy	round	sick	cold	long

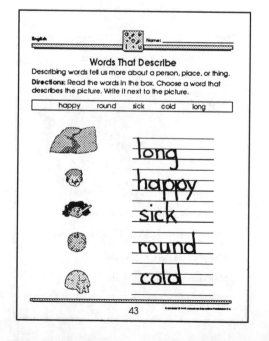

long

happy

sick

round

cold

Names Of People

The names of people begin with a capital letter.

Directions: Choose a name from the box to go with each child. Write the name on the line. Start each name with a capital letter.

Sam	Fred
Jack	Lisa
Ann	Jenny

ANSWERS VARY

1. Sam   4. Lisa

2. Ann   5. Fred

3. Jack   6. Jenny

Name That Cat

The name of a pet begins with a capital letter.

Directions: Read the names in the box. Choose one name for each cat. Write the name in the space under the cat.

Fritz	Fuzzy	Boots	King	Queenie	Lola

Queenie King Fuzzy

choices vary

Boots Fritz Lola

47

Holidays

Holidays begin with capital letters.

Directions: Choose the words from the box to match the holiday. Write the words under the picture. Be sure to start with capital letters.

Fourth of July	Valentine's Day
President's Day	Thanksgiving

Thanksgiving President's Day

Valentine's Day Fourth of July

48

Days of the Week

The days of the week begin with capital letters.

Directions: Write the days of the week in the spaces below. Put them in order. Be sure to start with capital letters.

Tuesday
Saturday
Monday
Friday
Thursday
Sunday
Wednesday

Sunday
Monday
Tuesday
Wednesday
Thursday
Friday
Saturday

49

Review

Directions: Circle the letters that should be capital letters. Underline the describing words.

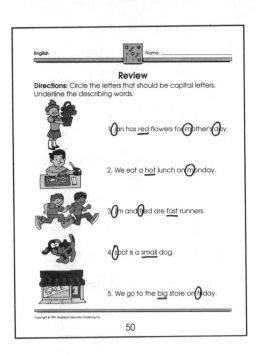

1. Jan has red flowers for mother's day.

2. We eat a hot lunch on monday.

3. Jim and fred are fast runners.

4. Spot is a small dog.

5. We go to the big store on friday.

50

Telling Sentences

Sentences can tell us something. Telling sentences begin with a capital letter. They end with a period.

Directions: Read the sentences. Draw a yellow circle around the capital letter at the beginning of the sentence. Draw a purple circle around the period at the end of the sentence.

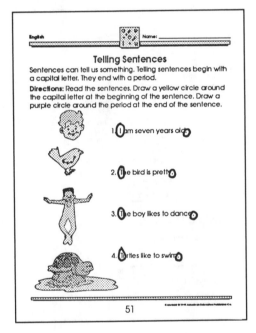

1. I am seven years old.

2. The bird is pretty.

3. The boy likes to dance.

4. Turtles like to swim.

51

Telling Sentences

Directions: Read the sentences. Write the sentences on the lines below. Begin each sentence with a capital letter. End each sentence with a period.

1. most children like pets
2. some children like dogs
3. some children like cats
4. some children like snakes
5. some children like all animals

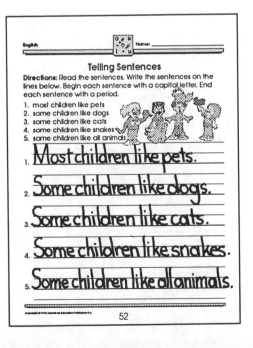

1. Most children like pets.

2. Some children like dogs.

3. Some children like cats.

4. Some children like snakes.

5. Some children like all animals.

52

81

Telling Sentences

Directions: Read the sentences. Write the sentences below. Start each sentence with a capital letter and end with a period.

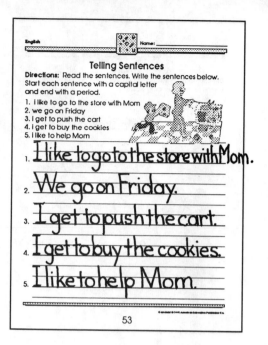

1. i like to go to the store with Mom
2. we go on Friday
3. i get to push the cart
4. i get to buy the cookies
5. i like to help Mom

1. I like to go to the store with Mom.
2. We go on Friday.
3. I get to push the cart.
4. I get to buy the cookies.
5. I like to help Mom.

53

Asking Sentences

Directions: Write the first word of each asking sentence. Be sure to start each question with a capital letter. End each question with a question mark.

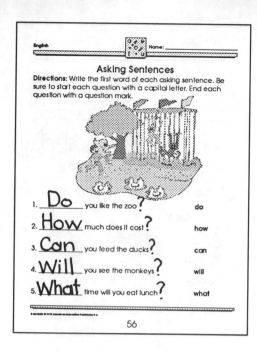

1. Do you like the zoo ? — do
2. How much does it cost ? — how
3. Can you feed the ducks ? — can
4. Will you see the monkeys ? — will
5. What time will you eat lunch ? — what

56

Asking Sentences

Asking sentences ask a question. An asking sentence begins with a capital letter. It ends with a question mark.

Directions: Draw a green line under the sentences that ask a question.

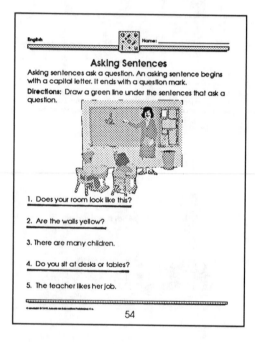

1. Does your room look like this?
2. Are the walls yellow?
3. There are many children.
4. Do you sit at desks or tables?
5. The teacher likes her job.

54

Periods And Question Marks

Use a period at the end of a telling sentence. Use a question mark at the end of an asking sentence.

Directions: Put a period or a question mark at the end of each sentence below.

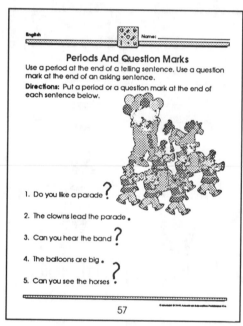

1. Do you like a parade ?
2. The clowns lead the parade .
3. Can you hear the band ?
4. The balloons are big .
5. Can you see the horses ?

57

Asking Sentences

Directions: Draw a blue line under the sentences that ask a question.

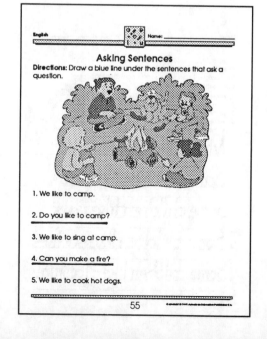

1. We like to camp.
2. Do you like to camp?
3. We like to sing at camp.
4. Can you make a fire?
5. We like to cook hot dogs.

55

Review

Directions: Look at the picture. In the space below, write one telling sentence about the picture. Then, write one asking sentence about the picture.

A telling sentence.

answers vary

An asking sentence.

58

Word Order

Word order is the logical order of words in a sentence.

Directions: Put the words in each sentence in order. Write the sentence on the lines.

1. We made lemonade. some
2. good. It was
3. We the sold lemonade.
4. cost it five cents.
5. fun. We had

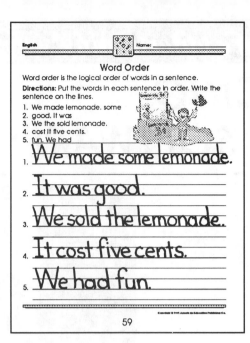

1. We made some lemonade.
2. It was good.
3. We sold the lemonade.
4. It cost five cents.
5. We had fun.

59

I Can Write Sentences

A story has more than one sentence.

Directions: Use the words from the pictures to write a story.

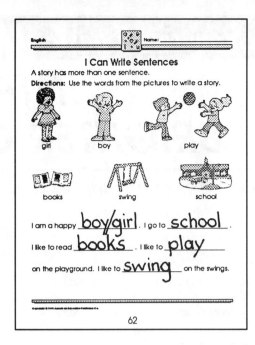

girl   boy   play

books   swing   school

I am a happy **boy/girl**. I go to **school**. I like to read **books**. I like to **play** on the playground. I like to **swing** on the swings.

62

Word Order

Directions: Look at the picture. Put the words in the correct order. Write the sentences on the lines below.

1. a Jan starfish. has
2. and Bill to Peg swim. like
3. The shining. sun is
4. sand. the in Jack likes play to
5. cold. water The is

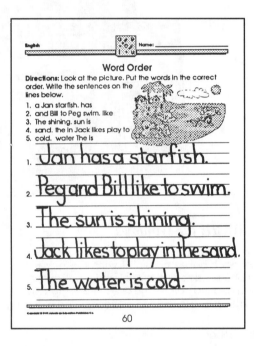

1. Jan has a starfish.
2. Peg and Bill like to swim.
3. The sun is shining.
4. Jack likes to play in the sand.
5. The water is cold.

60

I Can Write Sentences

Directions: Draw a picture of yourself in the box marked **Me**. Then write three sentences about yourself on the lines.

Me

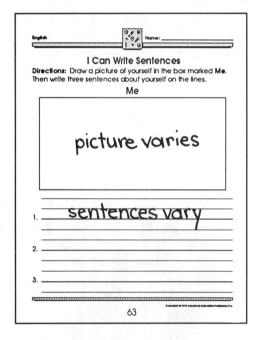

picture varies

1. sentences vary
2.
3.

63

Word Order Can Change Meaning

If you change the order of the words in a sentence, you can change the meaning of the sentence.

Directions: Read the sentences. Draw a purple circle around the sentence that describes the picture.

Example:

(The fox jumped over the dogs.)
The dogs jumped over the fox.

1. The cat watched the bird.
   The bird watched the cat.

2. The girl looked at the boy.
   The boy looked at the girl.

3. The turtle ran past the rabbit.
   The rabbit ran past the turtle.

61

Review

Directions: Put the words in the right order to make a sentence. The sentences will tell a story.

1. a gerbil. has Ann
2. is The Mike. named gerbil
3. likes eat. Mike to
4. play. to Mike likes
5. happy a is gerbil. Mike

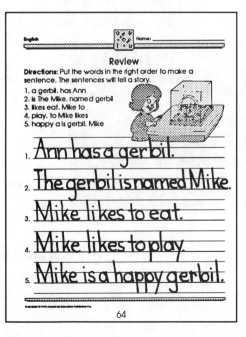

1. Ann has a gerbil.
2. The gerbil is named Mike.
3. Mike likes to eat.
4. Mike likes to play
5. Mike is a happy gerbil.

64

Now teach basic skills in a more entertaining way!

INTRODUCING
BRIGHTER CHILD™ *SOFTWARE!*

BRIGHTER CHILD ™ *SOFTWARE for Windows*

These colorful and exciting programs teach basic skills in an entertaining way. They are based on the best selling BRIGHTER CHILD™ workbooks, written and designed by experts who are also parents. Sound is included to facilitate learning, but it is not nesessary to run these programs. BRIGHTER CHILD™ software has received many outstanding reviews and awards. All Color! Easy to use!

The following programs are each sold separately in a 3.5 disk format.

Reading & Phonics Grade 1   Reading Grade 2   Reading Grade 3
Math Grade 1   Math Grade 2   Math Grade 3

CD-ROM Titles!

These new titles combine three grade levels of a subject on one CD-ROM! Each CD contains more than 80 different activities packed with colors and sound.

Reading and Phonics Challenge - CD-ROM Grades 1, 2, 3
Math Challenge - CD-ROM Grades 1, 2, 3

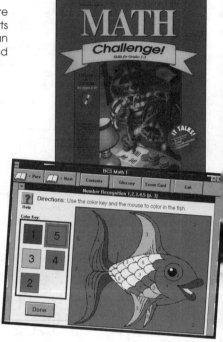

JIM HENSON'S MUPPET™/
BRIGHTER CHILD™ *SOFTWARE for Windows*™

Based on the best selling Muppet Press™/BRIGHTER CHILD™ Workbooks, these software programs for Windows are designed to teach basic concepts to children in preschool and kindergarten. Children will develop phonics skills and critical and creative thinking skills, and more! No reading is required with a sound card -- the directions are read aloud. The Muppet™ characters are universally known and loved and are recognized as having high educational value.

The following programs are each sold separately in a 3.5 disk format.
Each package contains:

- a program disk with more than 15 full color animated interactive lessons!
- sound is included which facilitates learning.
- Full-color workbook

Beginning Sounds: Phonics   Letters: Capital & Small
Same & Different

CD-ROM Titles

Beginning Reading & Phonics- CD-ROM

This title combines three different MUPPET™/BRIGHTER CHILD™ Software programs -- Beginning Sounds: Phonics, Letters, and Same and Different -- all on one CD-ROM! This valuable software contains more than 50 different activities packed with color, sound, and interactive animation!

Reading & Phonics II- CD-ROM

Three Muppet™ Early Reading Programs on one CD-ROM. Includes *Sorting & Ordering, Thinking Skills,* and *Sound Patterns: More Phonics*

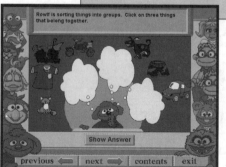

Available at stores everywhere.

Copyright© 1995 Jim Henson Productions, Inc. JIM HENSON INTERACTIVE, MUPPET PRESS, MUPPETS, MUPPET KIDS, and character names, likenesses and personalities are trademarks of Jim Henson Productions, Inc.

Microsoft is a registered trademark and Windows and the Windows Logo are tradmarks of Microsoft Corporation.

OVERVIEW

ENRICHMENT READING is designed to provide children with practice in reading and to increase students' reading abilities. The program consists of six editions, one each for grades 1 through 6. The major areas of reading instruction--word skills, vocabulary, study skills, comprehension, and literary forms--are covered as appropriate at each level.

ENRICHMENT READING provides a wide range of activities that target a variety of skills in each instructional area. The program is unique because it helps children expand their skills in playful ways with games, puzzles, riddles, contests, and stories. The high-interest activities are informative and fun to do.

Home involvement is important to any child's success in school. *ENRICHMENT READING* is the ideal vehicle for fostering home involvement. Every lesson provides specific opportunities for children to work with a parent, a family member, an adult, or a friend.

AUTHORS

Peggy Kaye, the author of *ENRICHMENT READING*, is also an author of *ENRICHMENT MATH* and the author of two parent/teacher resource books, *Games for Reading* and *Games for Math.* Currently, Ms. Kaye divides her time between writing books and tutoring students in reading and math. She has also taught for ten years in New York City public and private schools.

WRITERS

Timothy J. Baehr is a writer and editor of instructional materials on the elementary, secondary, and college levels. Mr. Baehr has also authored an award-winning column on bicycling and a resource book for writers of educational materials.

Cynthia Benjamin is a writer of reading instructional materials, television scripts, and original stories. Ms. Benjamin has also tutored students in reading at the New York University Reading Institute.

Russell Ginns is a writer and editor of materials for a children's science and nature magazine. Mr. Ginn's speciality is interactive materials, including games, puzzles, and quizzes.

WHY ENRICHMENT READING?

Enrichment and parental involvement are both crucial to children's success in school, and educators recognize the important role work done at home plays in the educational process. Enrichment activities give children opportunities to practice, apply, and expand their reading skills, while encouraging them to think while they read. *ENRICHMENT READING* offers exactly this kind of opportunity. Each lesson focuses on an important reading skill and involves children in active learning. Each lesson will entertain and delight children.

When childen enjoy their lessons and are involved in the activities, they are naturally alert and receptive to learning. They understand more. They remember more. All children enjoy playing games, having contests, and solving puzzles. They like reading interesting stories, amusing stories, jokes, and riddles. Activities such as these get children involved in reading. This is why these kinds of activities form the core of *ENRICHMENT READING.*

Each lesson consists of two parts. Children complete the first part by themselves. The second part is completed together with a family member, an adult, or a friend. *ENRICHMENT READING* activities do not require people at home to teach reading. Instead, the activities involve everyone in enjoyable reading games and interesting language experiences.

NEW! From the publishers of the acclaimed Master Skills Series

THE GIFTED CHILD ENRICHMENT READING AND ENRICHMENT MATH FOR GRADES 1-6

An exciting workbook series designed to challenge and motivate children...
the perfect complement to the Master Skills Series!

ENRICHMENT Reading is designed to provide children with practice in reading and to enrich their reading abilities. The major areas of reading instruction – word skills, vocabulary, study skills, comprehension, and literary forms – are covered as appropriate at each grade level. ENRICHMENT Reading is unique because it helps children expand their skills in playful ways with games, puzzles, riddles, contests, and stories. 64 pages plus answer key. Perfect bound.

ENRICHMENT Math was developed to provide students with additional opportunities to practice and review mathematical concepts and skills and to use these skills at home. Children work individually on the first page of each lesson and then with family members on the second page. At each grade level ENRICHMENT Math covers all of the important topics of the traditional mathematics curriculum. Each lesson is filled with games, puzzles, and other opportunities for exploring mathematical ideas. 64 pages plus answer key.

EACH BOOK IN THE 12 TITLE SERIES INCLUDES:

- 72 pages (64 lesson pages, 8 pg. answer key)
- Table of contents
- Games, puzzles, riddles, and much more!
- Perfect Binding
- Notes to parents
- Additional teaching suggestions
- Perforated pages

Only $4.95 Each!
AMERICAN EDUCATION PUBLISHING
America's Most Innovative Workbook Publisher

150 E. Wilson Bridge Rd. • Columbus, Ohio 43085

Page 65   Words and pictures will vary.

Page 66   *Mom:* mirror, map *Dad:* pajamas, pen *Pat:* bank, book *Bill:* ball, doll

Page 67   *Possible words:* lap, lip, dig, rib, cap, fan, fin, map

Page 68   Words will vary.

ENRICHMENT ANSWER KEY
Reading Grade 1

Page 69   Results will vary.

Page 70   Game of checkers will vary, but students
should know all the words.

Page 71   Answers will vary.

Page 72   *Words with same meanings:* little–small, silly–
funny, below–under *Words with opposite
meanings:* happy–sad, on–off, more–less,
nice–mean, up–down; winner will vary